ENGINEERING THE HUMAN BODY
ARTIFICIAL JOINTS

by Marne Ventura

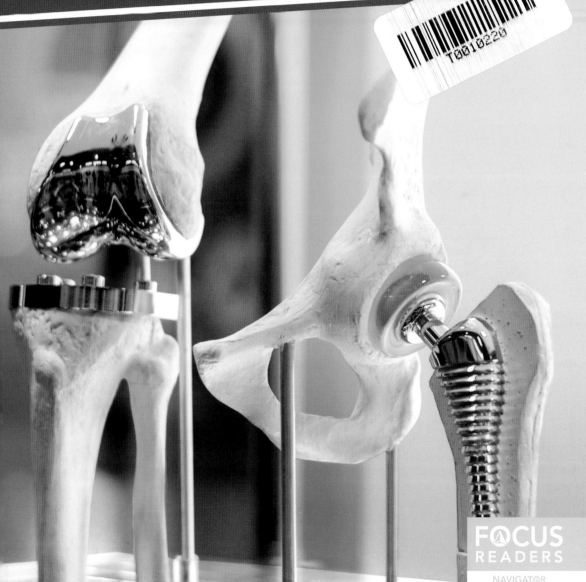

FOCUS READERS

NAVIGATOR

WWW.FOCUSREADERS.COM

Focus Readers is distributed by North Star Editions:
sales@northstareditions.com | 888-417-0195

Produced for Focus Readers by Red Line Editorial.

Content Consultant: Farshid Guilak, Professor of Orthopaedic Surgery, Washington University in St. Louis and Shriners Hospitals for Children–St. Louis

Photographs ©: Monstar Studio/Shutterstock Images, cover, 1; Phil Swallow/Shutterstock Images, 4–5; Wayhome studio/Shutterstock Images, 7; Jovanmandic/iStockphoto, 9; Jan-Otto/iStockphoto, 10–11; Oleksandr Malysh/Shutterstock Images, 13; Dr. P. Marazzi/ Science Source, 15; 33karen33/iStockphoto, 16–17; Denis Simonov/Shutterstock Images, 19, 24–25; Jarva Jar/Shutterstock Images, 21; itsmejust/Shutterstock Images, 23; Astrid & Hanns-Frieder Michler/Science Source, 27; Tek Image/Science Source, 28

Library of Congress Cataloging-in-Publication Data
Names: Ventura, Marne, author.
Title: Artificial joints / by Marne Ventura.
Description: Lake Elmo, MN : Focus Readers, [2020] | Series: Engineering the
   human body | Audience: Grades 4 to 6. | Includes bibliographical
   references and index.
Identifiers: LCCN 2019002985 (print) | LCCN 2019005474 (ebook) | ISBN
   9781641859684 (pdf) | ISBN 9781641858991 (ebook) | ISBN 9781641857611
   (hardcover) | ISBN 9781641858304 (pbk.)
Subjects: LCSH: Artificial joints--Juvenile literature. |
   Prosthesis--Juvenile literature. | Implants, Artificial--Juvenile
   literature.
Classification: LCC RD756 (ebook) | LCC RD756 .V46 2020 (print) | DDC
   617.4/72--dc23
LC record available at https://lccn.loc.gov/2019002985

Printed in the United States of America
Mankato, MN
May, 2019

ABOUT THE AUTHOR

Marne Ventura has written nearly 80 books for kids. A former elementary school teacher, she holds a master's degree in education from the University of California. Marne and her husband live on the central coast of California.

TABLE OF CONTENTS

CHAPTER 1

RESTORING MOVEMENT

Michael Rix was running 120 miles (193 km) a week. He was training for long races. Then his left hip began hurting all the time. One morning, he could not even put on his socks.

A surgeon said Rix had a disease of the hip joint. A joint is a place in the body where two or more bones meet.

People around the world run for fun, exercise, or competition.

Joints allow movement such as running. The surgeon said he could replace Rix's worn-out hip joint. He could put in an **artificial** joint.

Rix loved running. He thought getting an artificial hip meant he could no longer run. But the surgeon surprised him. Rix

TYPES OF JOINTS

Some joints move. Others do not. Fixed joints join the skull bones. These bones do not move. Knees and elbows are hinge joints. They work like a door that opens and closes. Hips and shoulders are ball-and-socket joints. The upper bone in these joints ends in a cuplike socket. The lower bone ends in a ball shape. The bones fit together at the joint. These joints move and rotate in many directions.

Running in the wrong shoes, on the wrong surfaces, or without proper warm-up can eventually lead to joint pain.

would not be able to run the longest races. But he could still exercise and run shorter races.

The surgeon removed the damaged part of Rix's hip. Then he put in an artificial hip covered in a ceramic coating.

Rix's bones **bonded** with the material. Soon he could leave the hospital.

In two weeks, Rix was riding an exercise bike. He could swim, too. Only three months later, he ran in a race. He beat 105 other runners. Three years after that, Rix won a silver medal at a worldwide sports competition.

Most people who get artificial joints are more than 60 years old. Older people are more likely to have joint diseases. Hips and knees are the most common joint replacements. Surgeons can also replace ankles, wrists, shoulders, and elbows.

At first, surgeons did not want to put these devices into younger people.

Joints wear out over time, making movement painful and difficult.

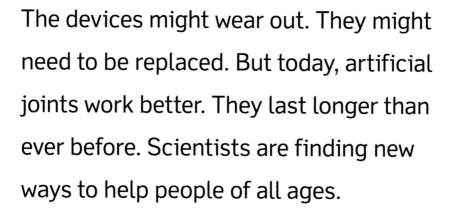

The devices might wear out. They might need to be replaced. But today, artificial joints work better. They last longer than ever before. Scientists are finding new ways to help people of all ages.

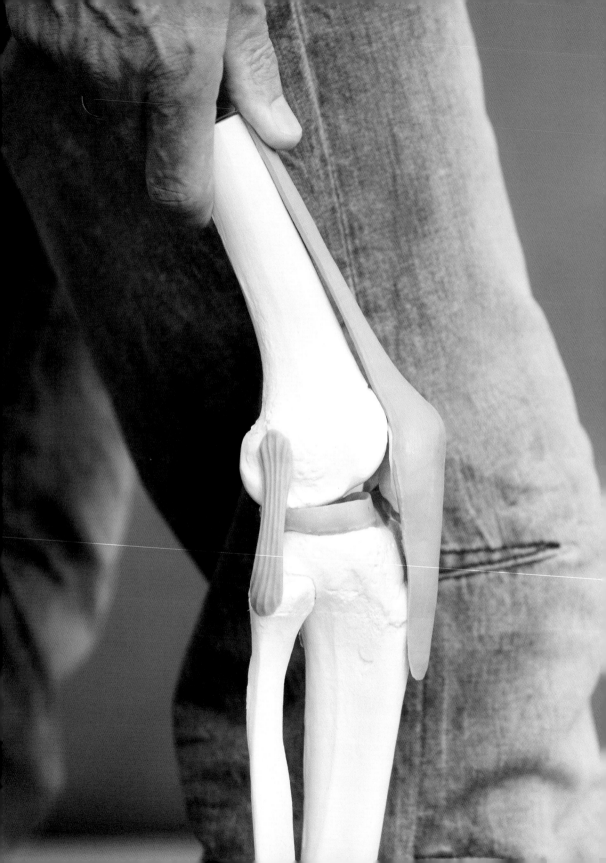

CHAPTER 2

IMPROVING THE DESIGN

Strong tissues connect the bones in a healthy joint. These tissues are called ligaments. Injury or overuse can cause them to tear. Torn ligaments can happen to people of all ages. They can cause great pain.

Other joint problems result from worn cartilage. Cartilage is a rubbery padding.

Ligaments are the tissues that hold joints together.

It covers the ends of the bones in healthy joints. It helps the joints move smoothly. Disease can cause this padding to wear down. Without the padding, the bones rub together. Pain and swelling occur at the joint. Many older people have pain because of joint disease.

PARTS OF JOINTS

Ligaments hold moving joints together. Ligaments are like thick rubber bands. They let the joint move. But they also keep it stable. Cartilage helps pad the bones in a joint. **Synovial** fluid fills the space between bones. It **lubricates** the joint. It is like the oil that helps a hinge work. Synovial fluid helps a joint move smoothly.

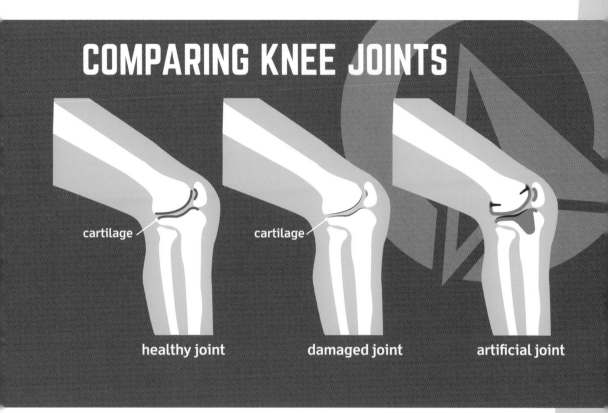

COMPARING KNEE JOINTS

cartilage — healthy joint

cartilage — damaged joint

artificial joint

People with diseased or damaged joints have trouble being active. They might not be able to play sports. They might not even be able to work. They can't get the exercise they need to stay healthy. They might have trouble sleeping.

Surgeons have been working on artificial joints for many years. In 1890, a German surgeon put an ivory knee joint in one patient. He put an ivory hip joint in another patient. He attached the joints to the patients' bones. He used screws and a type of glue.

These **implants** worked for a while. But in time, they caused **infections** in the joints. The surgeon wrote about his findings. He showed that bones fuse with artificial joints if glued together. He also recognized the need to find materials that would not cause infections.

In the early 1960s, a surgeon designed a new artificial hip. It had a plastic socket

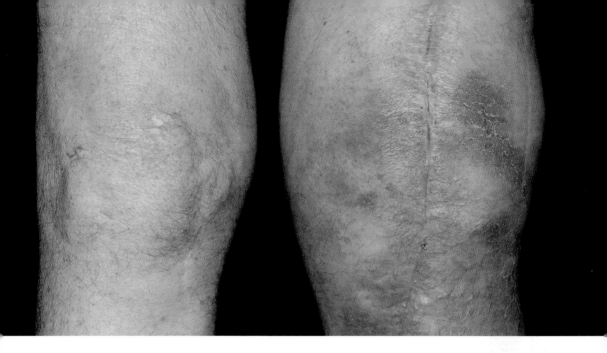

Infection can cause a joint to swell up. Joint infections can be very painful.

and a metal ball on a stem. The surgeon applied a bone glue used by dentists. This design worked better than previous ones.

Surgeons continue to try new designs and materials. Some designs are all metal. Some use plastic or ceramic. Some don't use any glue. These efforts have helped improve artificial joints.

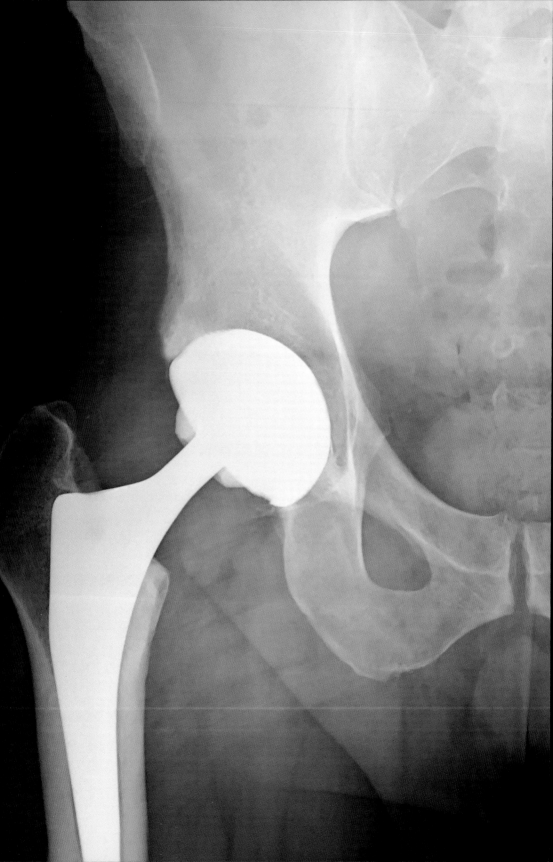

CHAPTER 3

JOINT REPLACEMENTS

Many diseases can affect joints. The most common joint disease is **osteoarthritis**. It mostly affects the knees and hips. They are the joints that move the most. They also bear the most weight.

The design of an artificial joint depends on the joint being replaced. Most artificial hips have two parts.

To treat osteoarthritis of the hip, surgeons may replace the hip joint with an artificial hip.

The first part is a metal stem with a ball on the end. The second part is a plastic socket. The surgeon puts the metal stem into the hollow leg bone. Then the surgeon attaches the plastic socket to the hip bone. In the past, surgeons needed to make a large cut to implant an artificial hip. Today, they only need to make one or two small cuts.

Surgeons can attach the artificial joint to the bones in two different ways. They can use a special cement. With it, they glue the joint to the bone. Or they can cover the metal piece with a ceramic material. This material **mimics** bone. After the joint surgery, the bones grow

An artificial hip joint mimics the appearance of a natural hip joint.

into this material. The artificial joint bonds to the bones.

The knee joint is where the thighbone, shinbone, and kneecap meet. Healthy knees can bend or straighten easily. The three bones move smoothly together. But the padding between them can wear out.

The bones rub together in a diseased joint. Surgeons cut out the damaged joint parts. They put in an artificial knee joint. Like hip joints, most artificial knees are made of metal, ceramic, or plastic.

Most patients who have joint surgery stay in the hospital for a week or less.

FINDING THE RIGHT MATERIAL

Scientists design joints to last as long as possible. For this reason, they need long-lasting materials. The right materials should not cause infection. They should not wear out. They should not lose their shape. They should move smoothly. Scientists have studied many different materials. The best options include metal, ceramic, and plastic. Metal and ceramic are hard. Plastic is tough and slick.

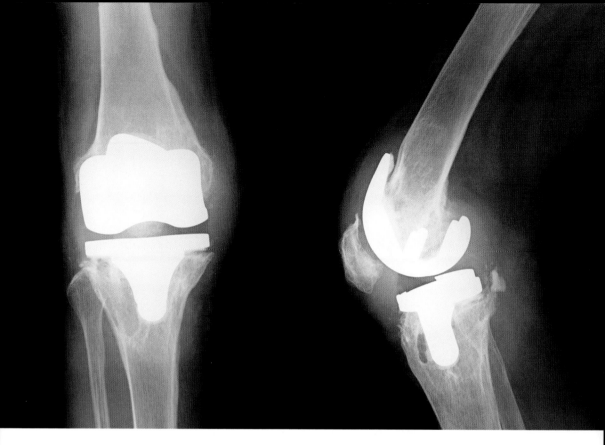

A surgeon attaches the parts of an artificial knee to the ends of the patient's bones.

They start to move around right away to exercise the joint. Patients start out with small, easy movements. Every day, they move a bit more. Most people can return to their daily activities within a few months.

WRIST REPLACEMENT

In plane joints, the sides of the bones are flat or curved. The bones slide against one another. The wrist is an example of a plane joint.

The wrist joint is made of eight bones. They are lined up in two rows of four. These bones connect to five bones in the palm of the hand. They also connect to two bones in the forearm. Tissues called tendons connect the arm muscles to the wrist.

Wrist joints can be damaged by overuse or injury. But surgeons can replace a wrist joint. First they make a cut on the back of the wrist. Then they move the tendons out of the way. They cut away the damaged joint surfaces. Next, an artificial joint is placed between the forearm bones and the hand bones. A plastic spacer keeps the artificial joint from rubbing against the bones.

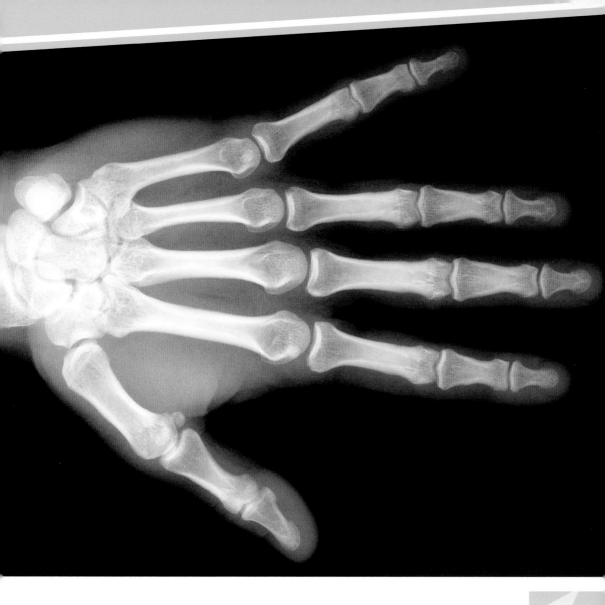

Many small bones make up the hand and wrist.

Surgeons repair and replace the tendons. Finally, they sew up the wrist. The patient wears a cast as he or she heals.

CHAPTER 4

FUTURE DEVELOPMENTS

Scientists are looking for new ways to make better artificial joints. Today's artificial joints typically last 20 years. New models might last longer. Young patients might be able to receive implants that last a lifetime.

Metal and plastic joints wear out over time. New models use different materials.

Artificial joints have improved greatly since the first models were created.

Michael Rix's artificial hip joint has a ceramic coating. The material is similar to a mineral found in human bone. The material causes the bone to grow into the artificial joint. This bonding keeps the new joint in place. Surgeons hope it will make the artificial joint last for the patient's entire life.

Some scientists are testing the use of bone or cartilage from **donors**. This method is different from putting in artificial joints. The donor joints would have all human material. Scientists are testing this method on dogs. They hope that in the future this method will be safe for humans.

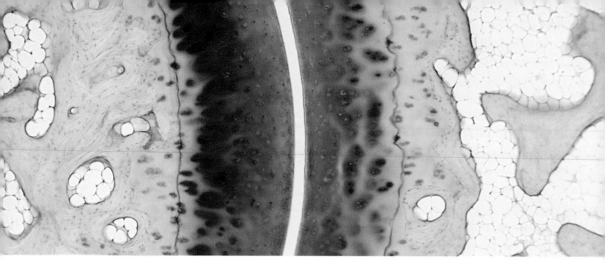

Cartilage (purple) pads the ends of healthy bones. Bones do not rub against one another in healthy joints.

One scientist is trying to use **stem cells** to grow new cartilage. He uses a 3D printer and other machines. He prints a woven fabric that will fit over a joint. Then he inserts stem cells from the patient's fat into the fabric. This fabric will be implanted into a diseased joint. The scientist hopes the stem cells will cause new cartilage to grow. The new cartilage would repair the damaged joint.

Researchers study stem cell treatments for bone disorders such as joint disease.

The patient would not need a metal and plastic replacement. However, more testing is needed before the surgery is ready for widespread use.

Scientists often use 3D printing to make artificial joints that fit the patient.

Joints that are custom-made fit better than standard, premade joints. Scientists are trying to develop better materials to use in 3D printers. They want materials that mimic human bone and cartilage. They hope these materials will cause the patient's joint to repair itself. The new cartilage might be able to fight off joint disease.

Technology has improved greatly since the first ivory hip joint in 1890. Artificial joints are lasting longer and working better. They are helping people move more easily and with less pain. Continued research will lead to even better artificial joints in the future.

FOCUS ON
ARTIFICIAL JOINTS

Write your answers on a separate piece of paper.

1. Write a letter to a friend describing what you learned about the different types of joints.

2. Do you think people with damaged joints should always get artificial joints? Why or why not?

3. Which joints are ball-and-socket joints?

   A. knee and elbow

   B. neck and spine

   C. hip and shoulder

4. What type of doctor would help a person with a damaged joint?

   A. a surgeon specializing in emergency care

   B. a surgeon specializing in heart health

   C. a surgeon specializing in bone health

Answer key on page 32.

GLOSSARY

artificial
Made by humans instead of occurring naturally.

bonded
Grew together and became attached on a molecular level.

donors
People who provide tissue or organs for transplant.

implants
Objects that are surgically placed in the body.

infections
Diseases caused by bacteria.

lubricates
Allows for smooth movement.

mimics
Copies an appearance or behavior.

osteoarthritis
A disease that causes the padding in joints to wear down.

stem cells
Cells that can divide and develop into
more-specialized cells.

synovial
Having to do with joints that move.

TO LEARN MORE

BOOKS

Beevor, Lucy. *Understanding Our Skeleton*. Chicago: Capstone, 2017.

Farndon, John. *Stickmen's Guide to Your Mighty Muscles and Bones*. Minneapolis: Hungry Tomato, 2018.

Morgan, Ben, and Steve Parker. *The Skeleton Book*. New York: DK Publishing, 2016.

NOTE TO EDUCATORS

Visit **www.focusreaders.com** to find lesson plans, activities, links, and other resources related to this title.

INDEX